Published in 2013 by The Rosen Publishing Group, Inc.
29 East 21st Street, New York, NY 10010

Photo Credits: **KEY** tl=top left; tc=top center; tr=top right; cl=center left; c=center; cr=center right; bl=bottom left; bc=bottom center; br=bottom right; bg=background

CBT = Corbis; DT = Dreamstime; GI = Getty Images; iS = istockphoto.com; PDCD = PhotoDisc; TF = Topfoto; TPL = photolibrary.com

front cover c TF; **2–3**tc GI; **4–5**cl TF; **6**bc, bl, br, cl TF; **7**cr iS; bc, br PDCD; bl, c, tr TF; **8**tl, tr TF; **8–9**br GI; **9**tr GI; **10–11**tr TF; **11**bc iS; br TF; **12–13**c TPL; **13**br, c CBT; **14**bl DT; **14–15**tr DT; **15**br CBT; **17**bc, cr CBT; cl iS; tr TF; **18**cl, cr, tl TF; **19**c PDCD; cr TF; **20–21**c TF; **21**c PDCD; tr TF; **22**cl iS; tr TF; **22–23**bc iS; **23**br, tr CBT; tc, tl TF; **24**cl, tc CBT; **24–25**c TF; **25**br CBT; **26–27**c iS; **26**tl TF; **27**br, c, tl, tr TF; **28**c, cl, cr, tl TF; **29**cl, cr, tl, tr TF; **30**c PDCD; **32**bg iS

All illustrations copyright Weldon Owen Pty Ltd.

Weldon Owen Pty Ltd
Managing Director: Kay Scarlett
Creative Director: Sue Burk
Publisher: Helen Bateman
Senior Vice President, International Sales: Stuart Laurence
Vice President Sales North America: Ellen Towell
Administration Manager, International Sales: Kristine Ravn

Library of Congress Cataloging-in-Publication Data

Brasch, Nicolas.
  Triumphs of engineering / by Nicolas Brasch. — 1st ed.
      p. cm. — (Discovery education: technology)
  Includes index.
  ISBN 978-1-4488-7887-1 (Library Binding) — ISBN 978-1-4488-7969-4 (pbk.)—
  ISBN 978-1-4488-7975-5 (6-pack)
  1. Buildings—Juvenile literature. 2. Engineering—Juvenile literature. I. Title.
  TA149.B726 2013
  620.003—dc23

2011051703

Manufactured in the United States of America

CPSIA Compliance Information: Batch #SW12PK: For Further Information contact Rosen Publishing, New York, New York at 1-800-237-9932

TRIUMPHS
OF ENGINEERING

NICOLAS BRASCH

PowerKiDS
press.

New York

Contents

Structures Around the World

Humans have an amazing ability to build the tallest, longest, largest, and most ornate structures imaginable. They have been doing so for thousands of years—think of the Egyptians and the pyramids. Some of these structures are very practical, while others are built just for their visual beauty. For whatever reasons they are built, there are many of these remarkable structures all around the world.

NORTH AMERICA

9

10

7

4

ATLANTIC OCEAN

2

SOUTH AMERICA

3

1 Channel Tunnel
Linking England and France, this tunnel was a joint project between the two countries.

3 Christ the Redeemer
Watching over Rio de Janeiro is this massive religious statue.

2 Panama Canal
This provides a shortcut between the Atlantic and Pacific Oceans.

4 Hoover Dam
Three US states receive the electricity provided by this dam.

10 Gateway Arch
This monument is the best-known image of St. Louis, Missouri.

ROPE

ASIA

PACIFIC
OCEAN

RICA

8

INDIAN
OCEAN

AUSTRALIA

5

9 Mount Rushmore
Four US presidents' faces are carved into rock in South Dakota.

...round the world

...bout every country in the world has amazing
...nade structures worth viewing and studying.
...nap shows where the ones on this page are located.

5 Sydney Opera House
Representing sails, this innovative building sits next to Sydney Harbour.

8 Petronas Towers
Located in Malaysia, these are the tallest twin buildings in the world.

7 Statue of Liberty
This statue was a gift to the American people from France.

6 Eiffel Tower
...ower is the best-known image of Paris, France.

1 Major breakthrough
The first major building milestone occurred in 1989. Construction workers, who had started tunneling at Folkestone, reached the coast of England at Dover, 5 miles (8 km) from their starting point.

2 Tunnel dimensions
Each of the three tunnels is 31 miles (50 km) long, and 24 miles (38 km) of t is under the sea. They sit 122 feet (40 below the seabed of the English Chann

Channel Tunnel

There were plans to build a tunnel between France and England from as early as 1802. However, wars and engineering problems saw these plans canceled until work started on the Channel Tunnel in 1987. The tunnel was officially opened on May 6, 1994. There are three tunnels—two carry trains and the other one is used to transport maintenance workers and vehicles. The Channel Tunnel links the towns of Folkestone, in England and Coquelles, in France.

St. Pancras International
The St. Pancras International station is the London terminal for Eurostar, the high-speed passenger rail service that travels via the Channel Tunnel between London and Paris.

3 Meeting halfway

On June 28, 1991, a giant drilling machine broke through the last section of rock, enabling French and British workers to shake hands. There was still three years of work before the tunnel would be ready for opening.

Since its opening, an average of 43,000 people have traveled through the tunnel every day.

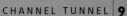

Panama Canal

The Panama Canal is a 50-mile-(80 km) long waterway that links the Pacific and Atlantic Oceans. Before it was built, between 1904 and 1914, ships traveling from one of the oceans to the other had to sail a long way around the southern tip of South America. Plans for a canal near Panama had been considered as early as the 1500s.

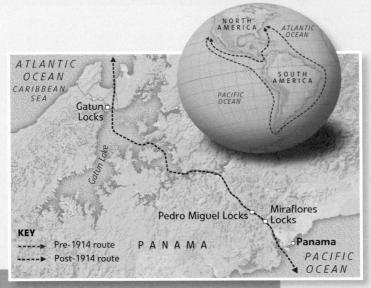

ATLANTIC OCEAN
CARIBBEAN SEA
Gatun Locks
Gatun Lake

NORTH AMERICA
ATLANTIC OCEAN
SOUTH AMERICA
PACIFIC OCEAN

Pedro Miguel Locks
Miraflores Locks

KEY
----▶ Pre-1914 route
----▶ Post-1914 route

PANAMA

Panama
PACIFIC OCEAN

A quicker route
It takes between 10 and 15 hours to sail through the Panama Canal, saving about 8,000 miles (12,875 km) and many days from a ship's journey from the east to the west coast of North America.

Canal locks
Three sets of locks raise and lower ships through the uneven land on which the canal is built. The Gatun Locks are near the entrance to the Atlantic Ocean and the Pedro Miguel Locks and Miraflores Locks are near the entrance to the Pacific Ocean.

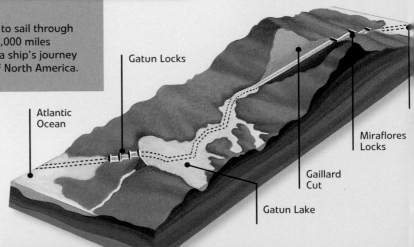

Gatun Locks

Atlantic Ocean

Miraflores Locks

Gaillard Cut

Gatun Lake

Raising and lowering

When ships enter the canal, the locks raise them from sea level (the Pacific or the Atlantic oceans) to the level of the Gatun Lake 85 feet (26 m) above sea level. They then lower the ships back to sea level to exit the canal.

The Culebra Cut

Almost 40,000 workers cut through forests, hills, and swamps to build the Panama Canal. The Culebra Cut was one of the most complicated. It involved laying and detonating explosives to loosen rock and clay, then using steam shovels to collect the rock and clay and haul it to dump sites.

Christ the Redeemer

Christ the Redeemer is a giant concrete and soapstone statue that overlooks the city of Rio de Janeiro, Brazil. It was built in the 1920s with money raised by the Catholic Church and, in 2007, was named one of the New Seven Wonders of the World. Weighing more than 660 tons (600 t), it stands 120 feet (38 m) high, while the arms span a distance of 98 feet (30 m).

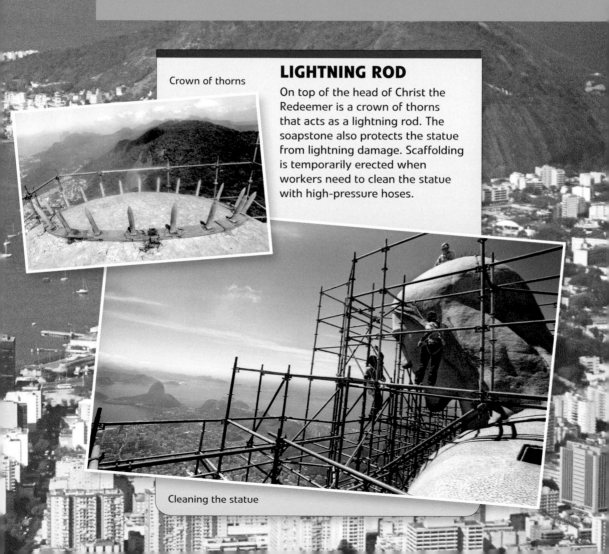

Crown of thorns

LIGHTNING ROD

On top of the head of Christ the Redeemer is a crown of thorns that acts as a lightning rod. The soapstone also protects the statue from lightning damage. Scaffolding is temporarily erected when workers need to clean the statue with high-pressure hoses.

Cleaning the statue

Dams

Dams are artificial barriers that divert water from their normal course. Sometimes this water is stored and other times it is diverted into different courses. Dams are built for several reasons: to prevent flooding; to store water for future need; and to generate electricity. While dams are very useful, they can be bad for the surrounding environment and for species that live in the water.

Hoover Dam
Located on the border of Nevada and Arizona, the Hoover Dam was built in the 1930s to divert water from the Colorado River to farms, as well as to generate electricity. More than 5 million barrels of cement were used to build the dam.

Three Gorges Dam
China's Three Gorges Dam is the largest electricity-generating plant in the world. It was a controversial building project because more than 1 million people had to move homes and several important environmental and archaeological sites were destroyed.

ou Dam
of the world's largest
oelectric dams is on the Paraná
on the border between Brazil
Paraguay in South America.
taipu Dam is 642 feet (196 m)
and 5 miles (8 km) long.

Sydney Opera House

The Sydney Opera House was built between 1963 and 1973, following an international design competition held in 1956. It was designed to blend into the harbor upon which it sits, with the roofs looking like sails. Today, the Sydney Opera House is one of the most recognized images of Australia and the major venue for classical music and opera in Sydney.

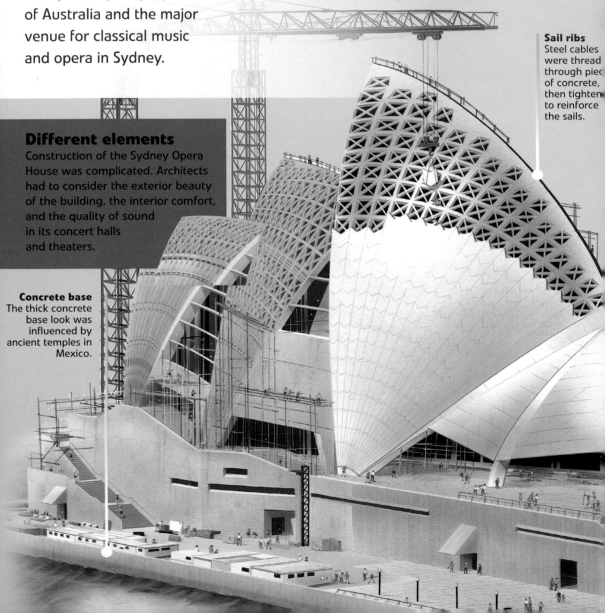

Sail ribs
Steel cables were thread through piec of concrete, then tighten to reinforce the sails.

Different elements
Construction of the Sydney Opera House was complicated. Architects had to consider the exterior beauty of the building, the interior comfort, and the quality of sound in its concert halls and theaters.

Concrete base
The thick concrete base look was influenced by ancient temples in Mexico.

JØRN UTZON

Arguments between the Danish architect, Jørn Utzon, and others involved in the building of the Sydney Opera House meant that progress was slow and difficult. In 1966, Utzon resigned from the project. However, in 1999, he agreed to design some changes to the building.

Inside the Opera House

There are six main performing and recording venues inside the Opera House, with the forecourt also used for performances. There are also restaurants, cafés, and function rooms. The building has World Heritage listing.

Main concert hall

The largest interior venue is the Concert Hall. It seats up to 2,679 people and has a concert platform up to 55.5 feet (17 m) wide and 36 feet (11 m) deep.

Tile construction

Specially made tiles were imported from Sweden. They were put together in panels on the ground, then lifted into place.

Glass windows

The walls and ceilings were constructed from glass that was made in France.

Opera theater

The opera theater can seat up to 1,507 people and accommodate 70 musicians in the orchestra pit. There are two elevators at the back of the stage that lift scenery up and down from the dock area below.

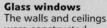

Restaurants and cafés

The complex has five restaurants and cafés, as well as several bars. The most recognized is Guillaume at Bennelong, an award-winning restaurant with stunning views of the harbor.

Eiffel Tower

The Eiffel Tower is the best known image of France, and more than 6 million people visit it each year. It was built in the 1880s to be the highlight of the 1889 World's Fair, held that year in Paris. The designer, Gustave Eiffel, was also the engineer. He had previously helped to construct the Statue of Liberty.

① **December 1887**

The tower's 18,000 separate elements were prepared in a factory on the outskirts of Paris, then transported to the site for erection. On December 7, 1887, the joining of the major girders up to the first level was completed.

② **May 1888**

The tower was assembled using wooden scaffolding and small steam cranes that were mounted onto the tower. As the tower got higher, the steam cranes moved up on runners that were eventually used for the tower's elevators.

③ **September 1888**

It took only five months to build all the pieces for the tower but 21 months to assemble them. The tower was completed on March 31, 1889. Not everyone in France supported the tower's construction, with many protesting against its "ugliness."

ttraction
ing 1,063 feet (324 m)
ne Eiffel Tower is about
me height as an 81-story
ng. There are elevators
e visitors to the top of
wer and 1,665 steps for
who prefer to walk.

THE WORLD'S FAIRS

The World's Fairs are public exhibitions that highlight scientific, industrial, artistic, and cultural achievements. The 1889 World's Fair in Paris attracted 28 million visitors during the six months it was open.

The dome of Machinery Hall, built for the fair, can be seen through the legs of the newly erected Eiffel Tower.

Statue of Liberty

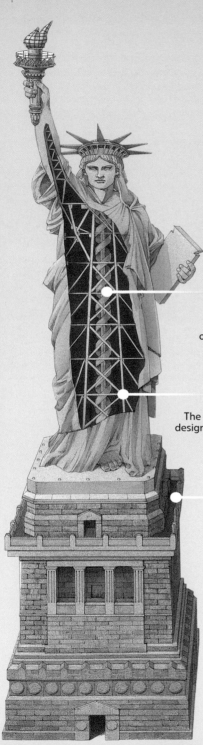

Since 1886, the Statue of Liberty has stood on Liberty Island in New York Harbor as a symbol of freedom an enlightenment. It was a gift to the American people from the people of France to mark 100 years of American independence in 1876. The statue was designed by Frenc sculptor Frédéric-Auguste Bartholdi.

Staircase
A spiral staircase with 354 steps leads to an observatory in the statue's crown. There is also an elevator for those who do not want to climb.

Supporting framework
The internal iron skeleton was designed by Gustave Eiffel, who designed the Eiffel Tower.

Pedestal
The pedestal on which the statue stands is made from granite.

Statue of Liberty
From the top of the pedestal to the top of the torch, the Statue of Liberty is 151 feet (46 m) high.

CONSTRUCTION
The Statue of Liberty was built in France, then packed into more than 200 crates and shipped to the United States, where it was assembled.

Designer Frédéric-Auguste Bartholdi (second from right) oversees the statue's construction.

Enlightening the world

The official name of the statue is "Liberty Enlightening the World." Liberty Island, where it stands, was previously known as Bedloe's Island. Nearby is Ellis Island, where immigrants were processed between 1892 and 1954.

Torch and crown

The torch is a symbol of enlightenment, while the seven points of the crown represent the seven continents. The tablet of law, held in the left arm, notes the date of American independence (July 4, 1776).

Mount Rushmore

The granite mountain in South Dakota into which the images of four famous presidents are carved, is known as the Mount Rushmore National Memorial. Attracting more than 2 million tourists each year, it was created by the American sculptor Gutzon Borglum, and was carved by several hundred workers between 1927 and 1941. The sculpted images stand 60 feet (18 m) tall.

Thomas Jefferson
Thomas Jefferson was the third US president. He wrote the Declaration of Independence, announcing the formation of an independent nation, and bought the Louisiana Territory from France in 1803, doubling the size of the country.

The site

The idea for a massive rock carving in South Dakota came from local historian Doane Robinson. He wanted images of local identities, however, and had a different mountain in mind. Gutzon Borglum overruled Robinson on both location and the identities.

George Washington
The first president of the United States was George Washington. He led the colonists against Britain in the American Revolution. His importance to the nation means he has the most prominent position on the mountain.

Construction

Before construction could begin, a stairway to the top of the mountain had to be built. Each morning, workers climbed the 700 steps to "clock in."

odore Roosevelt
he 26th US president,
odore Roosevelt
rsaw a period in the
y 1900s when the United
es became the world's
t powerful nation. He
membered as being
to both business and
king people.

Abraham Lincoln
As the 16th US president, Abraham Lincoln managed to hold the nation together during the Civil War. Another great achievement was abolishing slavery. Lincoln was the first US president to be assassinated.

Blasting the rock
Most of the work involved planting sticks of dynamite and blasting the rock. Drills were then used to define the facial features. The drilling process was known as honeycombing because of the pattern created by the holes.

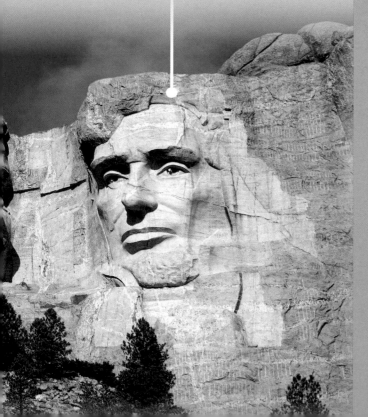

Hard at work
About 400 people were involved in building the monument. Many worked in boxes that were attached to thick steel cables, then lowered over the front of the 500-foot-(152 m) face of the mountain.

CONSTRUCTION OF THE ARCH

Although designed in 1947, construction on the Gateway Arch did not start until 1963. More than 5,000 tons (4,500 t) of steel and 38,000 tons (34,000 t) of concrete were used to build the arch and its foundations. The interior is hollow, allowing a tram to run through it.

Nearly finished
The final keystone was lifted into place on November 1, 1965. Each of these pieces weighed 10 tons (9 t).

Precision
The two legs were built separately, then joined. Measurements had to be perfect or they would not have matched up correctly.

Gateway Arch

The tallest manmade monument in the United States is the Gateway Arch in St. Louis, Missouri. It was built to honor US president Thomas Jefferson and the role that St. Louis played in the expansion of the country to the west. It was designed by the architect Eero Saarinen and took two and a half years to build.

Perfect curve

The Gateway Arch has the shape of a catenary curve, which is the shape formed by a free-hanging chain. It is 630 feet (192 m) high and exactly the same distance between the feet of the arch. Each leg has 1,076 steps.

View from inside

Visitors can peer over St. Louis from inside the arch. The Gateway Arch is hit by hundreds of lightning bolts each year but has lightning rods on top to prevent damage to the arch.

Skyscrapers

Tall buildings reaching toward the sky are called skyscrapers. The first were built in Chicago and New York City from the 1880s onward. Before then, the technology to construct tall, safe buildings did not exist. These two cities were perfect for skyscrapers because they were becoming heavily populated, and people and businesses needed new places to live and work.

Chrysler Building

One of the best examples of art deco architecture, the Chrysler Building in New York City opened in 1930. It was the tallest building in the world for one year, until the Empire State Building was opened.

Taipei 101

The world's tallest building from 2004 to 2010 was Taipei 101 in Taipei, Taiwan. It is 1,667 feet (508 m) from the ground to the tip of the spire, and 1,437 feet (438 m) from the ground to the highest occupied floor.

Burj Khalifa
In 2010, Burj Khalifa in Dubai, UAE, became the tallest building in the world. While it was being constructed it was called Burj Dubai. It is 2,717 feet (828 m) high and its elevator rises at a speed of 59 feet (18 m) per second.

pire State Building
n 1931 to 1972, New York City's pire State Building was the tallest ding in the world. Amazingly, ok only one year and 45 days uild, with the building rising stories per week for some of time. It has 1,860 steps.

30 St. Mary Axe
Also known as the Gherkin because of its distinctive shape, this London building has been designed to use as little artificial light as necessary inside. Despite its curved appearance, only one pane of glass is curved.

Petronas Twin Towers
Completed in 1998, the Petronas Twin Towers in Kuala Lumpur, Malaysia, are the world's tallest twin buildings. The designer was influenced by Islamic geometry and architecture, and the towers represent both Malaysia's culture and its future.

Time Line of Modern Wonders

The world's major cities look very different now th they did a century ago. This is because of improvements in technology and because peopl have come up with more exciting and inventive ideas Some of the resulting structures appeal to the eye, but others are far more practical.

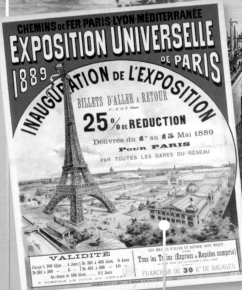

1886
The Statue of Liberty was opened in New York Harbor on October 28, 1886. The French and American flags were flown to reflect both the origin and the final destination of the statue.

1889
Posters promoting the 1889 World's Fair in Paris featured the newly opened Eiffel Tower as one of the highlights. The tower has been the most recognizable symbol of France since that time.

1914
Once the Panama Canal opened on August 15, 1914, boats could travel between the Atlantic and Pacific Oceans without having to journey around Cape Horn, the southern tip of South America.

1931
The Empire State Buil is a 102-story skyscra located on 5th Avenue and 34th Street in Ne York City. At the time it was built in 1931, it towered above the ot buildings surrounding

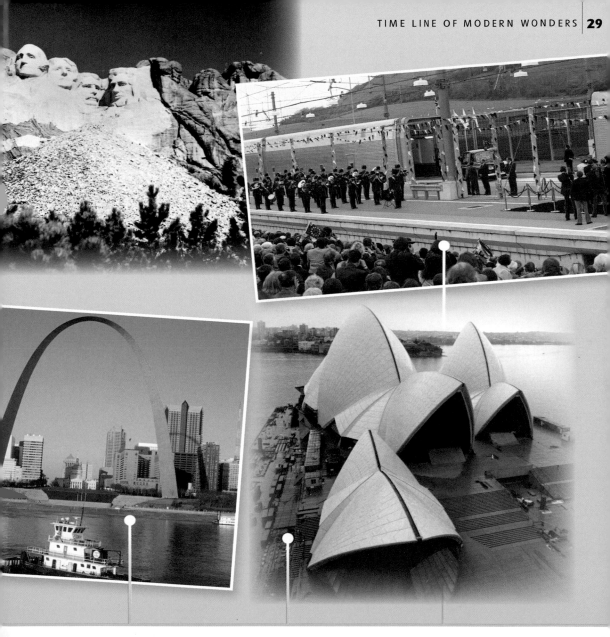

1965
The Gateway Arch on the banks of the Mississippi River in St. Louis, Missouri, was completed in 1965. It was designed as a monument to St. Louis' role in the opening up of the American west

1973
The Sydney Opera House in Australia was officially opened in 1973 by Queen Elizabeth II of Britain, Australia, and other Commonwealth countries. The Opera House took 15 years to build.

1994
The Channel Tunnel linked the countries of Britain and France for the first time. It was officially opened on May 6, 1994 by Britain's Queen Elizabeth II and the French president François Mitterand.

t Rushmore in
Dakota features
ulpted images of
S presidents. Since
veiling in 1941, it
ecome one of the
tourist attractions
country.

Build Your Own Structure

You have seen how some of the cleverest minds have designed and built structures that stretch human imagination. Now, it is your turn to put your thinking cap on.

What to do:

1 Think of a purpose for your structure:
- Is it to look good?
- Is it to link two places?
- Is it to honor an event or person?
- Is it to be the biggest or tallest of its kind?

2 Think of where it is going to be built:
- In your neighborhood?
- In your country?
- In another country?

3 Start drawing. Use your imagination.

4 Once you have drawn your structure, you can build it using cardboard, tape or glue, and scissors.

What you need:
- ☑ Paper
- ☑ Pencil
- ☑ Ruler
- ☑ Cardboard
- ☑ Tape or glue
- ☑ Scissors

lossary

tificial (ar-tih-FIH-shul)
ade by humans; not natural.

mplicated
OM-pluh-kayt-ed) Difficult.

ntroversial
on-truh-VUR-shul)
escribes something that
eates arguments.

etonating
EH-tuh-nay-ting) Exploding.

vert (dih-VERT) To redirect.

rder (GUR-der) A beam
sually made from steel, stone,
wood) that is used to support
rt of a structure.

hydroelectric
(hy-droh-ih-LEK-trik) Describes
electricity created from the
force of running water.

innovative
(IH-nuh-vay-tiv) Original.

keystone (KEE-stohn)
A wedge-shaped stone that locks
the parts of an arch together.

lock (LOK) Part of a waterway
in which boats are raised or
lowered by raising or lowering
the water level.

maintenance
(MAYN-teh-nins) Repairs.

pedestal (PEH-duhs-tul)
The base on which a statue
stands.

prominent
(PRAH-mih-nent) Important or
easy to see.

scaffolding (SKA-fohld-ing)
A series of poles, bars, and
platforms put together to
support people working above
the ground.

soapstone (SOHP-stohn)
A soft rock made up mainly of
the mineral talc.

span (SPAN) The distance
from one end to the other
of something.

structure (STRUK-chur)
Something made up of a number
of parts.

Index

Websites

Due to the changing nature of Internet links, PowerKids Press has developed an online list of websites related to the subject of this book. This site is updated regularly. Please use this link to access the list: www.powerkidslinks.com/disc/engine/